Troll First-Start® Science

This easy reader contains only 71 words, repeated often to help the young reader develop word recognition and interest in reading.

a	fair	rain	tiny
air	flat	raining	to
all	fog	rises	today
and	from	rushes	tomorrow
are	has	see	too
around	heat	shapes	us
be	hot	sizes	warm
close	in	snow	warms
cloud	is	snowing	water
clouds	it	some	weather
cold	kinds	sun	what
come	made	sunny	when
cool	make	tell	white
dark	makes	that	whoosh
do	much	the	will
draws	of	there	windy
drops	puffy	they	you
earth	puts	this	

Weather

by Melissa Getzoff
illustrated by Susan T. Hall

Troll Associates

Library of Congress Cataloging-in-Publication Data

Getzoff, Melissa.
    Weather / Melissa Getzoff; illustrated by Susan T. Hall.
       p.   cm.—(First-start science)
       ISBN 0-8167-3607-3 (lib. bdg.)   ISBN 0-8167-3608-1 (pbk.)
       1. Weather—Juvenile literature.   [1. Weather.]   I. Hall, Susan
T., ill.   II. Title.   III. Series.
QC981.3.G48   1994
551.5—dc20   94-26982

Copyright © 1995 by Troll Associates, Inc. All rights reserved. No part of this book may be reproduced or utilized in any form or by any means, electronic or mechanical, including photocopying, recording, or by any information storage and retrieval system, without written permission from the publisher.

Printed in the United States of America.

10 9 8 7 6 5 4

What is the weather today?

Is it sunny?

Is it raining?

Is it windy?

Is it snowing?

Is it hot?

Is it cold?

There are all kinds of weather.

What makes the weather?

The sun, air, and water all make the weather.

The sun warms the air around the earth.

When the sun warms the air, the air rises.
When the warm air rises, cool air rushes in.

That makes it windy. Whoosh!

The heat of the sun draws water from the earth, and puts it in the air.

This makes clouds.

Clouds come in all shapes and sizes.
What shapes do you see?

Clouds are made of tiny drops of water.
They tell us what the weather will be.

Some clouds are puffy and white.
The weather will be fair!

Some clouds are flat and dark.
There will be rain!

Some clouds are close to the earth.
This is fog.

When a cloud has too much water,
it will rain.

When the water in the cloud is cold, it will snow.